I0752567

IT'S
OKAY
TO BE
ME
Written by
Dr. Aundrea Mack Larrymore
Iván Larrymore II
Illustrated by
Kinnlik

ISBN: 979-8-9946307-0-9

Published by Larrymore Legacy Publishing
Printed in the United States of America

Library of Congress Control Number:
A Cataloging-in-Publication (CIP) record for this book has been applied for.

To my beloved son, Iván "Deuce" Larrymore II,

You are a living testimony of the beautiful and intentional way God designs each of us. From the very beginning, formed in my womb, He set you apart for a purpose all of your own.

"Before I formed you in the womb I knew you, before you were born I set you apart."

~Jeremiah 1:5

Your light shines with a brilliance in its own, illuminating the truth that different is not less; just divine. Your uniqueness, your rhythm, your voice, and your wonder are daily reminders that God does not make mistakes. He makes miracles.

This book is for you and every child like you, who sees the world through a different lens. May you always know that your story matters, your presence is powerful, and your life is wrapped in the most profound love a mother can hold.

With all my heart,

"Mommy" Aundrea Mack Larrymore

Autism Awareness & Acceptance

Some days feel loud.
Some days feel new.

But every day,
I’m proud to be...ME!

Sometimes I like quiet.
Sometimes I like sound.

I might spin or flap.
When I'm feeling joy
all around.

And it’s okay to be me.

I might not always look
Right into your eyes,

But I see you,
And I feel your heart right
by mine.

And it’s okay to be me.

I may need some space
or a big tight hug.

I show love
in my own way,
With a smile or a tug.

And it's okay to be me.

Sometimes I feel big feelings
And don't know what to do.

But with deep breaths
and kind words,
I can find my calm too.

And it's okay to be me.

I learn things my way,
Maybe slower, maybe fast.

But every step I take
Is one that will last.

And it's okay to be me.

I might not like changes
That happen too quick.

A plan or a picture
Can help things click.

And it's okay to be me.

Some friends like talking,
Some friends like play.

I like both,
But maybe in
a different way.

And it's okay to be me.

When I feel confused,
Or if things go all wrong,

I know I can try again,
And that makes me strong.

And it's okay to be me.

I'm brave, I'm kind.
I'm learning every day.
I shine like the stars,
In my own special way.

I'm not trying to be you,
And you're not trying to be me.
Because the best thing I can be,
Is wonderfully, perfectly ME!

About the Author

Dr. Aundrea Mack Larrymore is an accomplished author, visionary businesswoman, Kingdom Ambassador, and transformational leader dedicated to faith, empowerment, and community impact. Born on historic St. Helena Island, South Carolina, and now residing in Elgin, South Carolina, she has established herself as a trusted voice in leadership development, mentorship, and purpose-driven entrepreneurship.

As the Founder of Larrymore Legacy Publishing, Dr. Larrymore has created a purpose-driven publishing company that amplifies powerful voices, preserves generational stories, and produces inspirational, educational, and faith-based literature that transforms families and communities. Through her platform, she empowers authors to share their stories with excellence, integrity, and a global impact.

Dr. Larrymore serves as an Ambassador for the Kingdom and is recognized for her ability to blend psychology-based leadership principles with business strategies. She assists individuals, leaders, and organizations in building emotionally healthy, purpose-driven systems that foster growth and sustainability. Currently, she is the District Functional Behavior Instructional Consultant and an appointed Commissioner for Parks and Recreation, where she advocates for wellness, inclusion, and community engagement.

Additionally, she is a District Liaison and Chair for the Special Olympics, championing access and opportunities for individuals with exceptional needs, as the founder and co-founder of various community and faith-based initiatives including Seed Sower International, Thy Kingdom Come Outreach Ministries, the Miss Exceptional Pearl Pageant. Dr. Larrymore is committed to building sustainable platforms that empower families, develop leaders, and uplift underserved communities.

As a sought-after speaker and prayer leader, Dr. Larrymore inspires audiences to pursue their purpose boldly, lead with integrity, and create generational impact. Her mission is clear: to leave a lasting legacy of empowerment, excellence, and transformation for generations to come.

About the Co-Author

Iván Larrymore, II is a bright and energetic first grader who loves learning, exploring, and creating. He has a special passion for math and enjoys building and designing new creations, always imagining how things work. Ivan proudly shares that when he grows up, he wants to become an engineer, so he can invent helpful things that make the world better.

He is the youngest member of the Young Men Social Club of St. Helena Island, South Carolina, where he is learning leadership, manners, and how to be a respectful young gentleman. Ivan is a first grade student where he continues to grow in knowledge and confidence. His favorite color is blue, and his cheerful personality shines through his kindness, curiosity, and willingness to try new things.

Iván loves outdoor activities, especially playing, exploring nature, and learning about the world around him. One of his favorite things to do is farming with his grandfather, where he enjoys planting, learning about crops, and helping care for the land.

With his big heart, bright smile, and curious mind, Iván is already planting seeds of greatness and looking forward to a future full of discovery and success.